nabokov, Escalator East to Edinburgh and **Hull Truck**
in association with **Watford Palace Theatre and
The Mercury Theatre Colchester**
present the world premiere of

YOUNG

PRETENDER

by E V Crowe

World Premiere: 4th August 2011

T0347797

Company

CHARLIE	**Paul Woodson**
DONALD	**Chris Starkie**
FLORA / KATIE	**Rebecca Elise**

Directed by	**Joe Murphy**
Designed by	**Joanna Scotcher**
Lighting Design by	**Jack Knowles**
Sound Design by	**Edward Lewis**
Assistant Director	**Kirsty Patrick Ward**
Production Manager	**Dan Palmer**
Stage Manager	**Ceri Payne**

Young Pretender was first performed at Underbelly Cowgate at the Edinburgh Festival Fringe, on 4th August 2011.

Young Pretender is produced by **nabokov**, Escalator East to Edinburgh and Hull Truck in association with the Watford Palace Theatre and the Mercury Theatre Colchester. Escalator are supported by Arts Council England, East.

The Company would like to thank:
Claudia West and all at Arts Council England, East; Anthony Roberts at Escalator; Andrew Smaje and Angela Stone at Hull Truck Theatre, Brigid Larmour, Mathew Russell and Stephanie Hay at Watford Palace Theatre; Dee Evans and Tony Casement at Mercury Theatre, Colchester; Giles Smart at United Agents, Theresa Hickey at CDA London; Maryam Hunwick at Hunwick and Hughes Ltd, Jeremy Brook at Jeremy Brook Ltd, Charlie Boddington, Dr Eveline Cruickshanks, Lottie Vallis, Emma Laugier, Paul Jellis, Jeremy Herrin, James Grieve and George Perrin at Paines Plough; members of the Advisory Board.

Rebecca Elise Flora / Katie

Rebecca trained at East 15 Acting School. On graduating she was chosen by the Old Vic Theatre to form a small collective of actors in the first year of their Old Vic New Voices Company.

Recent theatre work includes: All Female Roles/Eric in *Baltimire* by Sandy Nelson (Oran Mor, Glasgow); Sophie Bruce in *Bear on a Chain* by Sue Glover (Oran Mor, Glasgow); Sarah in *Meeting Matthew* by Clive King and Hilary Brooks (Oran Mor, Glasgow); Doris in *Apeneck Sweeney* (Arches Theatre, Glasgow) and various new work at the Traverse Theatre, Old Red Lion Theatre and Theatre503 @ the Latchmere, London.

Film work includes: *Bulb* (Scottish BAFTA Award Winner for New Talent Scottish Screen/UK Film Council/GMAC); *Hysteria* (Scottish Screen); *Players* (Scottish Screen).

Recent radio work includes: *Realm of the census* (BBC Radio 4) and *The Penalty* (BBC Radio Scotland).

Chris Starkie Donald

Theatre credits include: *Black Watch* (National Theatre of Scotland & International Tour); *Peter Pan* (National Theatre of Scotland); *Knives in Hens* (BAC); *Borough Market* (Edinburgh Festival); *Last Train to Nibroc* (Orange Tree Theatre); *De Montfort* (Orange Tree Theatre); *Macbeth* (English Theatre Company); *Gladiator Games* (English Theatre Company); *The Knave in Grain* (Shakespeare's Globe Theatre); *Baghdad Wedding* (Soho Theatre).

Television credits include: *Walter's War* (BBC 4).

Film credits include: LIVE! (Essential Cinema).

Paul Woodson Charlie

Paul trained at Guildhall School of Music and Drama, where he received the Gold Medal Award. He previously worked with nabakov, performing at the Latitude Festival in the musical *It's About Time*. Other theatre credits include: *Merry Wives of Windsor* (Shakespeare's Globe Theatre, US and UK tour); *Romeo and Juliet* (Shakespeare's Globe Theatre and tour); *As You Like It*, *We that are left* (Watford Palace Theatre); *Three Sisters* (Lyric Theatre Hammersmith) and *Twelfth Night* (Tricycle Theatre). Television credits include: *Day Of the Triffids* and the forthcoming ITV drama *Eternal Law*.

E V Crowe Writer

E V Crowe has an MA in Creative Writing from UEA. She's a graduate of the Royal Court Theatre YWP. She has been on attachment to the Royal Court Theatre and National Theatre Studio. Plays include: *Kin* (Royal Court); *Live Feed* (ROTOR Siobhan Davies Studios); *Doris Day* (Soho Theatre/Clean Break); *A Just Act* (Clean Break); *Number 1* and *Community Hall* (Bush Theatre, Wraparound response and Election short); *One Runs the Other Doesn't* (Royal Court Rough Cuts). She is currently developing a new play for the Schauspiel Theatre, Frankfurt.

Joe Murphy Director

Joe is the Artistic Director of nabokov.

Theatre as Director includes: *The Boy on the Swing* (Arcola Theatre); *Bunny* (Edinburgh Fringe Festival and National Tour); *The Right Thing* (Liverpool Everyman/Election Special); New Short Plays by Jack Thorne, James Graham, Joel Horwood and Penelope Skinner (Bush Theatre); *Service*, *Building Site* (Arcola Theatre/Miniaturists); *After*, *Come on Over* (Tristan Bates); *The Things That Never Grew in the Garden* (Hampstead Start Night); *Normal* (Cockpit); *Julius Caesar*, *Esme-Tales* (Edinburgh Fringe Festival) and *South Pacific* (Northcott).

Theatre as Associate Director includes: *Punk Rock* (Lyric Theatre Hammersmith and tour); *The Laws of War* (Royal Court).

Theatre as Resident Director includes: *Ghost Stories* (Duke of York's, West End).

Theatre as Assistant Director includes: *Much Ado About Nothing* (Shakespeare's Globe Theatre); *The Priory* (Royal Court); *2nd May 1997* (Bush Theatre/Royal Exchange Theatre, Manchester); *Fixer* (High Tide Festival); *Purgatory* (Arcola Theatre); *Girls and Dolls* (Old Red Lion) and *He Said...* (Bush Theatre).

Joanna Scotcher Designer
Joanna completed a graduate design apprenticeship with
the Royal Shakespeare Company. She received the 'Best Set
Designer' award at the 2011 Whatsonstage Awards for her
site specific design of *The Railway Children* at the abandoned
Eurostar terminal at Waterloo station, London.
As well as the theatrical stage, her work has specialised in
promenade and site responsive design, spaces from the epic to
the intimate. Design credits include: *Blowing* (Fanshen, UK Tour);
The Caravan (Royal Court); *Counted?* and *The
Roundhouse History* (The Roundhouse, West Yorkshire Playhouse,
Latitude Festival); *Economy* (BAC); *Platform* (The Old Vic
Tunnels); *The Railway Children* (Waterloo and Toronto); *Inches
Apart* (Old Vic New Voices Award at Theatre503); *Cardboard
Dad* (Sherman Cymru); *Wagstaffe* (Mercury Theatre); *Paradise*
(Sheffield Crucible Theatres); *The Spidermen* (National Theatre,
Cottesloe).
Joanna is committed to producing exciting new design for
performance. www.joannascotcher.com

Jack Knowles Lighting Designer
Jack trained at Central School of Speech and Drama.
Recent lighting design credits include: *Victoria* (Arts Ed); *The
Boy on the Swing* (Arcola Theatre); *Imperial Fizz* (Assembly
Rooms, Edinburgh); *Room* (Tron Theatre); *One Thousand Paper
Cranes* (Imaginate Festival); *My Name Is Sue* (Soho Theatre &
UK tour); *If That's All There Is* (UK & International tour); *Red Sea
Fish* (59E59, New York); *Hanging By a Thread* (UK tour); *Love's
Labyrinth* (Opera Restor'd); *The Dragon of Wantley* (Potsdam
Schloss Theater); *A Guest for Dinner* (Arts Depot).
Associate/Assistant credits include: *Die Wellen* (Waves,
Shauspielhaus Koeln); *5 Guys Named Moe* (TRSE); *Something
in the Air* (Galeri); *Al Gran Sole* (Salzburg Festival); *Chodzenie
to Siberia* (30 Bird); *Origins* (Pentaus); *After Dido* (Young Vic);
...Sisters (The Gate Theatre).

Edward Lewis Sound Designer

Edward studied Music at Oxford University and subsequently trained as a composer and sound designer at the Bournemouth Media School. He has worked on numerous theatre productions, as well as for film, television and radio. Recent theatre work includes *On The Rocks*, *Amongst Friends* and *Darker Shores* (Hampstead Theatre); *Slowly*, *Hurts Given and Received* and *Apple Pie* (Riverside Studios); *Measure For Measure* (Cardiff Sherman); *Emo* (Bristol Old Vic and Young Vic); *I Am Falling* (Sadler's Wells and Gate Theatre); *The Stronger*, *The Pariah*, *Boy With A Suitcase*, *Le Marriage* and *Meetings* (Arcola Theatre); *Hedda* and *Breathing Irregular* (Gate Theatre); *Madness In Valencia* (Trafalgar Studios); *The Madness Of George III* and *Macbeth* (National Tours); *Othello* (Rose Theatre, Bankside); *Love*, *Question Mark* (New Diorama); *Knives In Hens* (BAC); *Personal Enemy* (White Bear Theatre and New York); *Accolade*, *In The Blood*, *The December Man*, *Beating Heart Cadaver* and *Mirror Teeth* (Finborough Theatre); *Quartet* (Old Vic Tunnels); *Kalagora* (National and International Tour); *Mad, Funny, Just* and *Mimi And The Stalker* (Theatre503). Edward has also worked on the Arden Project for the Old Vic and the Vibrant season at the Finborough Theatre.

He was recently nominated for an Off West End Theatre Award, and his films have won several awards at the LA International Film Festival and Filmstock International Film Festival. Edward also works as a conductor and music critic.

Kirsty Patrick Ward Assistant Director

Directing credits include: *The Baron* (Old Vic New Voices/Winner of Time Warner Ignite: 4); *Present : Tense* (nabokov/Watford Palace Theatre); *Take Heart* (Writers Rapid Response/Theatre503); *People Like Us* (Old Vic : New Voices/Vineyard Theatre, New York); *Life Support* (Catapulting Cocoon/York Theatre Royal); *Circular Doorways* (33% London Festival/Oval House Theatre); *Merry Christmas Joe* (Love Bites/Calder Theatre Bookshop); *The Return* (The Best of Love Bites/Southwark Playhouse); *The Sock* (nabokov/Watford Palace Theatre); *Seventeen Years, Ten Months & Twenty Nine Days* (First Time Voters Project/Bush Theatre).

Assistant Director includes: *The Boy On The Swing* (Arcola Theatre); *Bunny* (Fringe First Winner/nabokov/Underbelly Edinburgh Festival 2010/Regional tour 2011); *50 Ways To Leave Your Lover* (Bush Theatre); *DryWrite Presents: The Irreverence of Joel Horwood* (The Hospital Club); *Sit Down Mum, I Have Something To Tell You...* (Drywrite/Bush Theatre).

Kirsty was selected to be part of the Old Vic New Voices TS Eliot US/UK Exchange 2011 and was shortlisted for the JMK Young Directors Award 2011.

nabokov

nabokov is a theatre company resident at Watford Palace Theatre, dedicated to making work in response to immediately relevant social and political themes.

nabokov is a forum for artistic collaboration and innovation, dedicated to cultivating a young audience and distributing work as widely as possible.

Since 2001 **nabokov** has hosted a vibrant Events Programme and toured premiere Flagship Productions developing some of the UK's leading emerging talent. Previous productions include the World Premieres of *Artefacts* by Mike Bartlett (Bush Theatre, National Tour, New York), *Terre Haute* by Edmund White (Trafalgar Studios, National Tour), *2nd May 1997* by Jack Thorne (Bush Theatre, National Tour) and, most recently, *Bunny* by Jack Thorne which opened at the Edinburgh Fringe in August 2010, won the coveted Scotsman Fringe First 2010 Award, and is currently touring nationally and to New York.

nabokov produces a varied programme for artist development: Our mission is to provide emerging artists in our home region and across the UK with a framework to forge relationships and innovate their practice.

"Proving that political drama does have a place in the 21st Century"
The List

nabokov continues this development through touring productions: From the work and collaborators identified through our events we commission exceptional new playwrights and produce their work with extensively toured, high-value productions.

nabokov puts the audience at the heart of its work: We are devoted to re-affirming theatre's position within the cultural landscape by cultivating crucial new, young audiences.

Alongside its own events and productions, **nabokov** curates, produces and hosts work at festivals and events including the Latitude Festival.

For **nabokov**:

Artistic Director	**Joe Murphy**
Executive Director	**Ric Mountjoy**
Producer	**Lucy Oliver-Harrison**
Associate Producer	**Paul Jellis**
Advisory Board	**Emma Brunjes, James Grieve, Imogen Kinchin and George Perrin.**

hello@nabokov-online.com / www.nabokov-online.com
twitter: @nabokovtheatre

"Gives you a masterclass in what can be achieved in regional theatre at its best"
Daily Telegraph, May 2011

Nearly 40 years ago, an advert appeared in *Time Out*: "Half-formed theatre company seeks other half." With the caveat that the "other half" must be willing to move to Hull, Mike Bradwell set out to establish one of the most innovative theatre companies in Britain.

Writers and directors such as Alan Plater and Anthony Minghella joined Hull Truck over the course of the next 12 years. But it was John Godber who became the key figure in Hull Truck's next 27 years. Touring his brand of theatre to great acclaim, and encouraging talents such as Richard Bean and Amanda Whittington, the company rose to new heights of both popularity and national importance. Today, the legacy of both Bradwell and Godber, together with all the artists and writers they have fostered, is the foundation of the company's new home, a brand new theatre, which opened in 2009.

Under the creative leadership of Andrew Smaje, the company is responding to the opportunity of an increased capacity across two theatre spaces, an extensive community engagement programme and the exciting journey to discover and develop the next generation of outstanding writers and theatre-makers at Hull Truck.

New writing is at the core of Hull Truck's work. It is truly a writers' theatre, with a mission to produce the work of living playwrights and to showcase work made by the very best contemporary theatre-makers. Recent productions or commissions by Hull Truck include plays by Tom Wells, Tom Wainwright, Lucinda Coxon, Anthony Weigh, Morgan Sproxton, Richard Vergette, Sarah Davies and Selma Dmitrijevic.

In the last few months our collaborators and partners have included Headlong, Rash Dash, Bolton Octagon, Bristol Old Vic, Greyscale, The Gate Theatre and nabokov.

We invest in today's artists. We celebrate new forms of theatre-making. We make theatre for today's audience.

For Hull Truck:

Chief Executive	**Andrew Smaje**
Literary Manager	**Nick Lane**
Creative Associate	**Morgan Sproxton**
Head of Creative Learning	**Mark Rees**
Creative Learning Officer	**Madeleine O'Reilly**
Head of Marketing	**Angela Stone**
Head of Production	**Fran Maskell**

www.hulltruck.co.uk / www.facebook.com/hulltruck
www.twitter.com/hulltruck

Watford Palace Theatre is a local theatre with a national reputation. Contributing to the identity of Watford and Hertfordshire, the Palace enriches people's lives, increases pride in the town and raises the profile of the area through its work. Watford Palace Theatre is the creative heart of Watford and a leading arts organisation in Hertfordshire.

Watford Palace Theatre is a 21st-century producing theatre - open to ideas, collaborative in approach, imaginative in its use of resources. Across artforms, a range of emerging and established artists are actively supported and genuinely nurtured, in an entrepreneurial environment combining flexibility with artistic rigour, with their work presented on our stage and screen and other spaces in the building and beyond.

We aim to engage with all the communities that surround us and create inclusive live and interactive experiences, developing a reputation for exceptional and diverse theatre. We produce high quality work that is distinctive and ambitious, embracing varied styles and cultures of theatre. This work attracts artists of stature to Watford and provides opportunities to nurture new and emerging artists.

As a charity we rely on funds from Arts Council England and Watford Borough Council. On top of this, we receive support from many local businesses and people who contribute to the work we do, so that we can continue delivering enjoyable, exhilarating and accessible productions on stage and beyond.

The Mercury Theatre Colchester is a highly respected regional theatre and home to the critically acclaimed Mercury Theatre Company, staging a broad mix of classic plays and new writing as well as working extensively within the local community. Described as "a really terrific regional theatre" (Guardian), in 2010 the Mercury staged the world premiere of King David Man of Blood, a new play by Fraser Grace, "a work of intelligence and audacity" (The Times). A venue for the best touring theatre and entertainment, the Mercury also provides a platform for local performing arts groups and artists.

Since 2003 the Company has built up a strong reputation and audience for new writing, collaborating with, amongst others, nabokov, Dialogue Productions, Real Circumstance, Tilted Productions, The New Wolsey Theatre, Wildworks, Scamp Theatre, The Bush Theatre, Soho Theatre and Watford Palace Theatre.

An International Festival at the Mercury in October 2011 presents three new plays created by artists from five different countries and a major co-production of Captain Corelli's Mandolin with the Kote Marjanishvili Theatre, Tbilisi and NFA International Arts and Culture.

For more information about the Mercury Theatre and Company please visit www.mercurytheatre.co.uk

YOUNG PRETENDER

E V Crowe

YOUNG PRETENDER

OBERON BOOKS
LONDON
WWW.OBERONBOOKS.COM

First published in 2011 by Oberon Books Ltd
521 Caledonian Road, London N7 9RH

A catalogue record for this book is available from the British
Library.

ISBN: 978-1-84943-179-8

Cover image by Graham Cheal.

For my friends

My unending gratitude to Giles Smart, Leo Butler, Purni Morell, Ruth Little, Jeremy Herrin, Amy Hodge, Shiv Malik, Megan Walsh, Ruth Fitzsimons, Foad Dizadji-Bahmani, Tamzin Robertson, Joe Murphy, Serina McDuff, Penny Skinner, Nick Payne, everyone at nabokov, Oberon Books and Watford Palace, the cast who performed the rehearsed reading, my parents, my sisters and rebels, revolutionaries, idealists and activists.

Characters

CHARLIE, 25

DONALD, 30

FLORA, 16

KATIE, 16

1. EDINBURGH

CHARLIE dances wildly and strangely.

DONALD watches from a distance with a drink.

CHARLIE stops. Breathes.

CHARLIE: My brother, Henry.
When we were younger he would write lists of the things he wants to do.
To get himself to become the person he imagines he could be – rounded, successful, hot.
I found one before I left. On his desk.
In a special leather notepad. Not one with lines. But graph paper.
And he doesn't tell anyone. He just writes the little list, beneath a little 'to do', underlined. Colon.

CHARLIE takes it out, reads it.

To do:
1. Learn a musical instrument. Eg. Lute
2. Study more.
3. Visit – (I can't read that one). Family, possibly.
4. Update music collection.
5. Go on more dates.
6. Go somewhere different every summer.
7. Read at least three of the classics.
8. Pray.
9. Take up running / lose weight.
10. Weigh myself weekly.
11. Get a haircut.
12. Be more interested in fashion.

Every time I find a list I lock him in the cupboard.
And when I let him out, he apologises.
Donald.
I'm back in that moment, when I first started having –

Real ideas, and people went 'he's cocky' or 'pushy',
'kidder' and *now* I'm standing, in real life on great solid
slabs of an-idea-come-to-fruition called 'Edinburgh victory'.
And I start thinking, so a bit more, a bit bigger, because
I can do it, I've done this. Nearly. If you listen, London's
whining for me. Donald, London's wet for me.
If I had a role model, it would be me.

Remembering the list.

Henry, I love my brother. He won't have done any of the
things on his list.
I have *one* thing.
I've told everyone I know, all my friends, everyone in
my family, all the people who know me that this is what
I'm going to do. This is who I am the person who does
this who impresses other people very suddenly and does
something really very remarkable. I've set a trap for myself
Invade Scotland and England.

He smiles.

Tick.

DONALD: Well –

2. CULLODEN

DONALD sits on a child's chair.

CHARLIE enters with a napkin under his chin.

DONALD removes the napkin, takes the dinner fork out of CHARLIE's hand.

KATIE comes in after him. Stands flat against the wall, staring at CHARLIE.

CHARLIE: I don't understand it.

Pause.

CHARLIE: I don't understand it.

DONALD wipes CHARLIE's mouth clean with the napkin.

CHARLIE: It's downstairs having dinner.

Pause.

CHARLIE: Chomping pork and potatoes.
Feeding itself.

DONALD: Kilravock?

CHARLIE: Just another old person.
Still alive.

DONALD: –

CHARLIE: He seems to think I want his advice.

DONALD: –

CHARLIE: Or his input.

DONALD: He did make us dinner.

CHARLIE: To stick his beak in.

DONALD: It's an opportunity.

CHARLIE: As if I'm looking for a mentor.
Or for guidance.

DONALD: He wants to help.

CHARLIE: I've got a track record!
The fuck.

DONALD: Aye. (*Summing up.*)
Edinburgh, no the castle
Very enthusiastic
Later, English Tories seem enthusiastic.
Bad times at Dumfries.
Wade-dodge at Carlisle
Manchester no Englishmen join. Some French do.

Deserters. We're down to five thousand.

At Derby, the English fuck us over. French get cold feet,
English Tories get cold feet. Repeat.

But for a moment, there is a moment of possibility, of…
London.

Then

Carlisle Castle – Jesus.

Murray extracts us back North!

Beg borrow steal in Dumfries.

Christmas, we're at sorry Glasgow

North! Stirling Castle no.

Now here.

– Your CV.

Pause.

CHARLIE: I don't understand it –
doubt.

KATIE goes.

Door slams.

DONALD: People don't know you that's all.

CHARLIE: I'm capable of a lot.
Kilravock! The doubter.
The fat doubter.

DONALD: He did make us dinner.

CHARLIE: You go back and fill your trough
like a senior citizen at a free buffet.
He's not a Jacobite.

DONALD: So?

CHARLIE: So don't be grateful. Or humble.
Don't say thanks. I have to watch your mouth well up
with deferential-slobber.
Go back in if you prefer…

Go and suck him off if you like.

DONALD: It's rude to just, leave the table.

CHARLIE: Me, I, yes, now, me, yes, now, I, me, yes.
There's nowhere to have a clear head.

CHARLIE checks there's no other way in or out of the room.

Peepholes everywhere for them to spy on us.
Old people are such perverts. Don't you think?

DONALD: I have a clear head.

CHARLIE: YEH! If only I'd known I'd end up fighting
next to a guy who sketches little wild flowers as we march
towards invasion.
(*Sarcastic.*) In a rebellion what you need most is someone
tender.
Who can see all the beauty there is in the world.
Did you see Kilravock? His face. His fat, fuck,
face. Like he's bored.

CHARLIE impersonates.

At the table, I talk, and his eyes... long shore drift.
You, silence of the lambs.

DONALD: –

CHARLIE: Me, I, yes, now, me, I, Jacobite hero.
He talks over me when I speak. I can't breathe in for fear
of him spleening chat, me inhaling his outhale.
He calls me Young Pretender like he's renaming a plant.

DONALD: He was playing with you.

CHARLIE: Ha, haaaaaaaaa.

DONALD: He's concerned.

CHARLIE: His face reminds me of my Dad.
Squished, and serious and disa-fucking-pointed.

23

Painfully disafuckingpointed. Before I've disappointed
anyone. It's IN ADVANCE.

DONALD: If Kilravock's advice is to speak with the English
General over dinner...

CHARLIE: Fuck yes, an instinctive bootlicker.

An archetypal happy peasant.

Someone they herd in with flowers in your hair

To dance and cheer at weddings.

They need you in the picture, you're an extra.

A cut out rainbow in the background.

Thank God you could make it along.

DONALD: I respect Kilravock that's all.

CHARLIE: For WHY? I want him to become interested in flora
and fauna.

DONALD: He thinks we're dead tomorrow.

CHARLIE: I want him to start gardening.

DONALD: He knows we're in retreat.

CHARLIE: –

DONALD: He wants to help us keep alive.

CHARLIE: He said 'pass me the salt, anarchist'.

DONALD: Talk to him.

CHARLIE: Only about geraniums. I don't talk politics with old
people.

DONALD: He thinks the weather will get worse tomorrow.

CHARLIE: Old people always say that. When he said the word
'revolution'

he went like this – (*CHARLIE does the sign for inverted commas
with his hands.*)

DONALD: –

CHARLIE: 'Kilravock'. I, me, yes, now.

DONALD: He's offering us a way out.

CHARLIE: Pensioner.

DONALD: It's not me, Charlie. It's you.
You made us stay here.
It seems like you want it to –
You wanted to talk.
If someone invites you to dinner you don't have to say
'shall I bring red or white?'

Pause.

DONALD: I'll tell them you're having a rest.

CHARLIE: Well no, I'm emotional.

DONALD: –

CHARLIE: Tell him that.
I'm unwilling to stay at the table to be served up a dialogue
with the enemy.
I'm pro childish outbursts.
I, yes, me, now, yes, now.
It's Kilravock shut the fuck up o'clock.

DONALD: –

CHARLIE: It's ok to *feel* it.

DONALD: I'm not like you.

CHARLIE: You should feel it.
If you feel it, you can't even look
at someone like Kilravock.

DONALD thinks.

CHARLIE: Kilravock's eyes on me…

DONALD: He thinks you're young that's all.

CHARLIE: (*Triumphant.*) I AM YOUNG.

Pause.

…Looking me all over.

DONALD: What would your Dad do…?

In a kind of physical pain.

CHARLIE: / Why do people want to talk about Dad? Dad?
Dad thinks there's a way of doing things. A way of
rebelling, properly. The Jacobite way –
Timing!
Boats!
Family!
Amazing!
The French!
Terrific!
The Hanoverians!

'As your Father, we can safely say, I think your revolution
will be shit'.
It won't be like that for us. We've got *newer* new ideas.

DONALD checks the door is shut.

Slam.

DONALD: I don't know Charlie.

CHARLIE paces.

CHARLIE: What?

DONALD: The movement.

CHARLIE: What?

DONALD: What if this is as far as we can push it?

CHARLIE: Culloden. The ride stops at Culloden?
I don't think so. No way.
We've got to get all the way to

London this time.

Recruit more men.

Go back to England and finish what we started.

We win here, and Scotland will hold.

We're on a roll.

Oh no, Donnie's got old man syndrome.

You're at the point when it feels more convenient to die than to bother finding clean underpants.

When we're fucked, I'll tell you we're fucked.

DONALD: We're FUCKED. We couldn't BE MORE FUCKED.

CHARLIE: I'm the fuckometer! ME.

DONALD: I had to STEAL boots from a village in Dumfries.

I took a pair off a man's feet in the middle of the street.

I watched him walk home bare foot.

That is not what I opted into.

Not this kind of experience.

CHARLIE: We're missing some this and that, but you know, we're young…

DONALD: The movement is –

CHARLIE: It's experimental.

DONALD: If it gets too much, you said, 'we can stop'.

CHARLIE: Who wanted to stop at Edinburgh?

You! Remember?

We won.

So cleanly.

You begged me not to storm it.

Then we licked it.

Whipped it.

DONALD: *Starting* is easy.

CHARLIE: Me, I, yes, now, I, yes, now, I, ME.

It doesn't even cross my mind that this isn't good
or right or the right thing to be doing.
I feel optimistic.

DONALD: You're an optimist! We're two to one, the rain is
supernova, you've walked out of a peace deal dinner
hosted by our only ally, our army is half dead. Joseph,
Edward, Richard, Hugo, William – our friends. We've left
them at the roadside like abandoned toys.

CHARLIE: They're people we know.

DONALD: When people first meet you they like you so much.
You're so convincing.

CHARLIE: That's interesting. What does that mean?

DONALD: Nothing.

CHARLIE: What?

DONALD: Nothing?

CHARLIE: Say it.

DONALD: I feel like…

CHARLIE: What?

DONALD: Nothing. (*Pause.*) You wooed me.

    Pause.

CHARLIE: (*Correcting.*) Recruited.

    Pause.

Look.
No one does this.
No one tries this.
We're achievers.
Gold star people.

DONALD: You're a fanatical.

CHARLIE: But it's true.

How liberating, right?

Just the truth:

– It's not fair.

– Our turn.

– Hand it over.

– Fuck off.

Our 'manifesto'.

DONALD: You used to have it all written down. More than that.

CHARLIE: Really?

DONALD: In your pocket.

CHARLIE checks his pockets.

CHARLIE: But this is much clearer.

DONALD: There was more than that. More to it. More – justification.

CHARLIE: Our subjugation, infantilisation, is justification enough.

Pause.

They make CHILDREN of us.

DONALD: We could tell all our friends 'go home'.

CHARLIE: Cripple!

DONALD: Listen…

CHARLIE: Dementia sufferer.

DONALD: We could tell our friends 'we're sorry, it's over'.

CHARLIE puts his thumb down at the idea.

CHARLIE: Grandpa.

DONALD: They don't have shoes.

CHARLIE: Fuss pot.

DONALD: Half our men don't have a sword to fight with.

CHARLIE: What's your point?

DONALD: It's not just Kilravock who thinks we'll lose tomorrow.

KATIE comes in, gives CHARLIE a message. He reads it.

DONALD: Is it from Henry?

CHARLIE tosses the paper, disappointed.

CHARLIE: The English General's arrived downstairs.

DONALD shifts the piece of paper with his foot. CHARLIE and DONALD think, unsure what to do, they look at KATIE.

KATIE: This house was built in 1553. This is going to be the new nursery. They've had problems with the roof. They're re-decorating.

CHARLIE: (*To DONALD, continuing his thoughts.*) My brother and I had a nursery until I was about twelve. By the time I was twelve I had things largely worked out and I've spent the next twelve years consolidating those ideas. I know I'm right.

Silence. KATIE fills the space.

KATIE: Someone told me there was going to be a festival outside, with music and games and fun things.

KATIE moves to leave.

CHARLIE: Tell them we need more time.

KATIE: Are the men camped outside part of the festival?

CHARLIE: They're part of the war.

KATIE: Against what? Fun?

CHARLIE: Against some English people. Some Scottish people.

KATIE: I like fun things.

Pause.

KATIE: What did you say your name was?

CHARLIE: CHARLIE. Bonnie Prince Charlie.

She shrugs.

Goes.

DONALD: He won't wait around for long.

CHARLIE: He'll wait.

DONALD: You agreed to talk. Kilravock made the invitation.

CHARLIE: They can see us.
Little peep holes in the walls.

DONALD: They can't.

CHARLIE: After tomorrow the whole world will know who
you are.

DONALD puts a thumb up.

CHARLIE: It's good for them to see you.
You look right.

DONALD: You said that before.

CHARLIE: People trust you.

DONALD: You said I look like a working man.

CHARLIE: A highlander!

DONALD: Now what am I?

CHARLIE: A revolutionary!

DONALD: You can't call yourself a revolutionary.
Someone else can label you a –

CHARLIE: *I'm* a revolutionary.

DONALD: It's more of a…'look' isn't it.

CHARLIE: What?

DONALD: It's for – . It's a style.

CHARLIE: For cool people?
We are cool.

DONALD: Farming sheep is real work…

CHARLIE: / Maybe if they were *your* sheeps.

DONALD: Sheep.

CHARLIE: Farming someone else's sheeps.
This is so you count your *own* sheeps at night…
wake up. Master of you.

DONALD: I had *something*.

CHARLIE: You didn't.

DONALD: My old life.

CHARLIE: I, me, yes, now, I, now, yes.

Pause.

DONALD: I called it 'duty' to my wife.

CHARLIE: Personal responsibility, good.

DONALD: And then I left.

CHARLIE: For a reason.
A CAUSE.

DONALD: I left them all alone.
For –

CHARLIE: For?

KATIE comes in.

KATIE: For someone called Charlie. A message from the
English General.

CHARLIE takes the note. She goes.

CHARLIE: Old man handwriting!

DONALD: What does it say?

CHARLIE: I can't read 'old man'.
Curly wurly letters. I think it says 'What will you do even if you win?'
Non capisco.
Aren't they supposed to…?
He thinks he can message me. As if I know him. It's an imposition. (*Shouting as if they can hear.*)
Annoying!
We're allowed to do this.
You're allowed to – criticize.
I don't have to know everything up front.
I ask questions, I'm the questioner!

DONALD: (*To pacify.*) This is our chance to be delicate. To keep our lives.
To save our men.

CHARLIE reads the note again.

CHARLIE: (*Addressing the General, standing on a chair.*) I, me, now, yes, now, I, me. Dear General… I'm a believer in the Jacobite dream! I want the English crown and government to FUCK OFF.
Donald, we can't go down and talk. There's nothing left to say, which is why they call it 'war' rather than 'afternoon tea' or dinner in this case. As if we would trade in a new dawn for roast pork.
We're him in ten years if we're not careful. On the payroll, gagged, self-serving, degenerate, sender of notelets.
What's his name? Geriatric general?

DONALD: The Butcher.

CHARLIE: ?

DONALD: That's what they call him.

CHARLIE: And I'm called Bonnie?

DONALD: He's very violent.

CHARLIE: Who Ok'd Bonnie?

DONALD: It's supposed to intimidate you.

CHARLIE: Shout out to him.
Tell him.

DONALD: Tell him what?

CHARLIE: Tell him.

DONALD: No.

CHARLIE: Tell him why you believe in the Jacobites.

DONALD: Why?

CHARLIE: Proclaim.

DONALD: It's not appropriate.

CHARLIE: Say it.

DONALD: I came because you asked me to.

CHARLIE: That's not true.

DONALD: It is true.

CHARLIE: You came because you personally believed in the possibility of change. Fuck. I want to hear it.

DONALD: OK...

CHARLIE: I've given you some balls and the Peak District. Fucking proclaim!

DONALD loses all energy.

DONALD: You promised me.

CHARLIE: –

DONALD: You said I wouldn't have to go back embarrassed.

CHARLIE: Say something.

DONALD: *This* is embarrassing.

CHARLIE: If you *feel* it.

DONALD: I *feel* you could have been better organized.

Silence.

DONALD: We don't have to risk it.

CHARLIE:

DONALD: What do we do if we lose?

CHARLIE: –

DONALD: What if Henry doesn't make it here in time?

CHARLIE: (*In pain.*) He will.

DONALD: What if you don't make it?

CHARLIE: Doubter! Doubter! Look, my family, the Stuarts, we don't give up on anything – international combat, warfare, hunting, charades. Fifty-seven years of Jacobite rebellion to return James VII of Scotland and II of England and subsequent descendents, ME! to the throne.
It's not an option. People like me don't lose. I honestly don't know any losers. And anyway, I've told everyone this is what I'm doing.
We're doing this. I listened to 'advice' about London. I heard you, you were wrong. What you needed was a strong decision from me not a team hug.

Pause.

CHARLIE: Imagine if you spent your whole life walking up and down the same hillock.
The English keep waltzing in
Putting your hair in bunches.

Licking your face.

Make being Scottish 'cute'.

Do you want people for hundreds of years dancing in pink kilts on special occasions, doing the wrong steps at a cèilidh? With someone *calling out* the right moves because they don't know them without instructions?

Whatever it is you love about your life, it's temporary.

You could lose it for being here yes.

But you'll definitely lose it up there giving oral sex to sheep while they fuck you over from behind.

DONALD: –

CHARLIE: Imagine being thirty and feeling you're floating.

Thirty is old enough to be engaged in the detail of living. In the admin, the small print. Because the people who wrote the detail, people like Kilravock, people like the General, already have everything they need because they were cleverer than us.

It's 1746.

We don't have time to fuck about.

DONALD: I am thirty.

CHARLIE: I thought you were younger.

Pause.

CHARLIE: Henry's bringing extra troops.

As soon as he gets here…

DONALD: There's nothing from him.

CHARLIE: Donald!

DONALD: I didn't say it.

CHARLIE: I could hear it from INSIDE you.

You wanted to say – I *doubt* he'll come.

DONALD goes.

KATIE opens the door, watches him, holding a note. CHARLIE turns eventually.

KATIE: From overseas.

CHARLIE: –

KATIE: Famous. You're famous.

CHARLIE: –

KATIE: Do you have a girlfriend?

CHARLIE takes the message.

KATIE: Everybody says – you're famous and you'll be dead tomorrow.

Pause.

With the weather and the marshes and the combat conditions.

CHARLIE: –

KATIE: Everybody says you're insane and you're addicted to drugs and you're crazy and you're going to walk thousands of men to slaughter and you've already lost and you're so completely fucked. I think it's amazing. The Jacobite cause is so cool. You're going to be mud wrestling out there in your own blood. Oh my god I can't believe it. Do you know what they're chanting outside –

CHARLIE: 'Alternative system of governance, alternative system of governance!'?

CHARLIE reads it.

She leans to touch him.

DONALD returns. She goes. DONALD stands near.

CHARLIE: Every time you breathe in, standing so close to me, it sucks a little more wind out of my sails.
He never even left France.

DONALD puts his hand on his shoulder.

CHARLIE: He wants to be here.
He lets Dad think I'm the bad one.
You see.
I'm – the let-down.

Pause.

Dad doesn't even know I smoke.

DONALD: Surrender us.

CHARLIE looks as though he might cry. He snaps out of it.

CHARLIE: The thing is… Kilravock has something we don't
have, we won't ever have… security. Basic security – an
income, somewhere to live, the facility to plan a family, a
holiday. These are the new luxuries.
How old were you when you met your wife?

DONALD: –

CHARLIE: And you have a daughter don't you?

DONALD: She's very precious.

CHARLIE: Pretty?

DONALD: She's very pretty and very precious.

CHARLIE: If we win.

DONALD: I only have one daughter.

CHARLIE: I see.

DONALD: –

CHARLIE: Why, is she a dog?

Pause.

CHARLIE: These things are important.

DONALD: We can talk about it.

CHARLIE: She must be really – precious.

Pause.

CHARLIE: Because I also want normal things.
Normal-normal. Sweet things. For me. (*He looks around.*) A
nursery.

DONALD: You want a family do you?!

CHARLIE: Yes.

DONALD: Really?!

CHARLIE: Everyone expects me to want to be famous or to
want to be un-normal. I'm fighting for normal things,
which unfortunately isn't normal. Right? But it doesn't
mean, I don't deserve good things. To have good things.
You know. Like 1) a family, 2) love.

Pause.

So

Pause.

CHARLIE: Maybe with you alongside me.
There's a kind of – shadow.
I don't feel like myself.

DONALD: Don't you Charlie?

CHARLIE: Before… it was more like a camping trip, with a
death toll.

DONALD: Charlie.

CHARLIE: But now, all this time with you. I feel old or
something.

DONALD: Charlie.

CHARLIE: And now they're calling me a crazy.

DONALD: This *was* crazy.

CHARLIE: IS crazy.

KATIE comes in. CHARLIE grabs her and pins her violently under with a chair against the wall.

CHARLIE: WHAT?!

KATIE: Message from the people outside, they're shouting out, all of them: 'Charlie, Charlie, Charlie!'

He lets her go.

CHARLIE: (*To DONALD.*) Get the General to delay a couple of days.
So we can wait for the French.

DONALD: –

CHARLIE: I've decided.

DONALD: It's too late.

CHARLIE: He came here to be nice.
Let him be nice.

DONALD: We can't act the insulted equal one minute and the prodigal son the next.

CHARLIE: I, me, now, yes.
Talk to him. Reason with him.
I won't let Culloden become another wimp out, another London.
This is our plan of action…

DONALD: We missed our chance. Kilravock set it all up.
You left the table.

CHARLIE: …Apologise if he heard me complain. Make me seem immature, or inexperienced.

DONALD: I'll do my best.

CHARLIE: Be receptive and open to his advice and ideas.
Look admiring of him.

Look upwards.

DONALD: I can try.
I can try to talk to him.

CHARLIE: Negotiate. Flatter.

DONALD stalls, afraid.

DONALD: I'm not very good at talking to people.

DONALD goes.

CHARLIE sits. Motionless.

After a while, DONALD comes back.

DONALD: He knows the French aren't coming, the English rebels aren't coming and another clan has left us. He wants to fight tomorrow. He's taking us seriously. He's gone to wake his men.

Silence.

DONALD: I could send out word for a western clan...

CHARLIE: Did you offer him any dessert? Ice cream?

DONALD: ...for help.

Pause.

CHARLIE: One thing and you're back in here.

DONALD: It would take days for them to join us.

CHARLIE: I asked *you.* One thing.

DONALD: I'm sorry.

Pause.

CHARLIE: I can't remember.
I feel like I just met you.

DONALD: We're friends.

CHARLIE: More...

DONALD: / You left the dinner. Insulted Kilravock, refused to respond to the General's messages.

CHARLIE: (*Correcting.*) More *comrades*.

DONALD: I did my best Charlie.
He's a serious man.

CHARLIE: *I'm* serious.

DONALD: The men are –

CHARLIE: I know what the boys are. The boys are my boys, and you are not my boy.

DONALD: Charlie. I am your boy.

CHARLIE: You're not my boy.

DONALD: I wouldn't agree.

CHARLIE: The only thing I've asked you to do you haven't done.

DONALD: I've done my best Charlie.

CHARLIE: Well.

DONALD: I've been devoted.

CHARLIE: You should have told me our situation was critical.

DONALD: I did!

CHARLIE: Not very confidently!

Pause.

CHARLIE: You know the difference between being a success and being a failure? Having one person who backs your decisions no matter what. And fresh air. (*Pause.*) Well I've had plenty of fresh air.

DONALD: It's me.

42

CHARLIE: –

DONALD: *I* back you.

> *DONALD approaches him. CHARLIE hugs him, kisses his cheek, DONALD relaxes, relieved.*

> *CHARLIE checks the walls.*

CHARLIE: Have I told you the story about... My Dad used to tell us this story. About a great warrior, a great rebel who trusted all of his men to uphold the values and ideals of the rebellion, and at all costs to win at all costs. Have I told you this...?

DONALD: No, no.

CHARLIE: Just when they thought all was lost, on the morning of the battle, his most trusted soldier took a tiny dagger, hidden and asked to surrender in person to the enemy General.
They took him into their ranks, unsuspecting.
And the soldier killed the General. Taking everyone by surprise.
And this is what happened.
I, me, now, yes.

DONALD: And then they killed the soldier.

CHARLIE: Yeah.

DONALD: They would.

CHARLIE: The enemy was greatly weakened without their General.
It was the right thing. No doubt.

> *Pause.*

DONALD: Did he write a goodbye letter to his wife?

CHARLIE: I don't think so.

DONALD: No?

CHARLIE: He was often unfaithful. Apparently.

DONALD: Oh, yes.

CHARLIE: He fell in love…

DONALD and CHARLIE: …easily.

CHARLIE: And then there just wasn't time for letter writing. All the ink and paper.

CHARLIE shrugs.

CHARLIE: Inspiring right?

DONALD: No one thought it was against the rules? Or dishonourable? Or not ok?

CHARLIE: He backed his leader.

All I know is he couldn't be dissuaded.
His commitment was such.

Pause.

I'll send her a postcard.

DONALD stands, lost.

OK?

They shake hands. DONALD reluctant to release.

DONALD: I feel like I've done all this the wrong way.

CHARLIE: Self doubt! The plague of our generation.

CHARLIE waits for DONALD to go.

DONALD: How old are you tomorrow?

CHARLIE: Twenty-five.

DONALD: Happy birthday then.

Not looking at DONALD, CHARLIE gives him the thumbs up.

DONALD goes.

CHARLIE looks round.

CHARLIE: Me. Twenty-four. Done.

CHARLIE sits, pulls out the napkin, examines it.

3. HIGHLANDS

CHARLIE is in his underpants. FLORA is at the wall.

She doesn't say anything for a while.

FLORA: Terrific.

Pause.

Terrific.
It's been.
Terrific.
They've kept coming.
To the door.
They don't use the –
They don't knock.
These people.
Terrific.
I didn't think you'd come.
You're here.
It's true.
It's like a miracle.
I've felt desperate.
Fuckin –
apprehensive.
Away with it.
On my own.
I've been going –
Fuckin –

CHARLIE: Where's your Mum?

FLORA: She's gone.

She left.

She went actually. So.

CHARLIE: Is she coming back?

FLORA: They don't usually.

Do you know what I mean?

They don't usually come back.

This is terrific.

Terrific.

It's terrific.

Pause.

Where's my pops?

CHARLIE: I wanted to talk to you both.

I came here to –

FLORA: Well she's no here.

You can talk to me.

You'll have to talk to me.

This is terrific.

I thought the only

Reason we would no ha' heard

A peep from yous. Or had a message

Or something is if we won and yous

Wanted to make it a big surprise

A big moment.

This is your big moment.

I expected you to look more

I expected –

You look terrific.

It's just.

A king.

If you're a king, ken.

Or a prince.

I don't know what these people
Supposed to look like.
But – you look.
You look terrific.
When you're out there.
Is there no a
Is there no a way to get word
Is there no a way to communicate
To let us know.
It's been a long time.
It's been terrific.
But we've been waiting.
I've been waiting by the door
For word.
And they come and tell me
Tha we've lost and now we have
To go.
We've got to leave the house.
They burned down the house next door.
It looks terrific.
Was there no a way to send a message to me
Did my Pops no message me?

CHARLIE: Sorry.

FLORA: I'm a Jaco. I don't mind
Saying that. I'm a Jaco.
I've been fighting on my own.
I feel like I've been fighting on my own.
To keep our own door.
It's terrific.
I've been trying to stand up
To stand, resilient or.
Like they teach us to.
Is this the big surprise,
Is this why I've no heard from my

Pops.
Is this the big surprise.
Say surprise.

CHARLIE: I wish I'd got here quicker.

FLORA: Surprise!

CHARLIE: Did anyone see me come in?
Because –

FLORA: There isn't anyone.
I can tell everyone.
There isn't anyone.
They've been cleared.
They've gone.
The rebellion.
It's terrific.
It's been terrific.
Did we win?
Congratulations.

CHARLIE: Do you have a blanket?

FLORA: No the black watch took them.

CHARLIE: Do you have a shirt?

FLORA: No the black watch took all the shirts.

CHARLIE: I need your help.
I feel quite –

FLORA: I can see you're –
Stay here.

FLORA comes back with a bundle.

CHARLIE puts on the dress.

You look terrific
It's terrific.

CHARLIE: I want to tell you about
Donald.
Your Pops.
I've walked a long way.

FLORA: I don't mind if he died and
We won. If he died and we won that's ok.
You're up here having a look.
You're up to see the land on foot.
It's terrific up here.
Did you see him go?
Was it terrific?

CHARLIE: No.
Yes.
From the corner of my eye.
He died fighting.

FLORA: Worth it then.
To win.
It was worth something.
It's terrific.
Was there blood everywhere?

CHARLIE: What?

FLORA: Did you see my Father's blood
spatter everywhere?
Did it splatter?
Did it get in anyone's eye?
Did his head come off?
Did they cut it off in the fight?

CHARLIE: A shock for you.

FLORA: I'd die like that.
If you believe in it, you have to be willing to die
For it.
Did other people die?

CHARLIE: They even murdered the injured.

FLORA: If it's worth it.
    People are going to get hurt.
    Arms and legs and tongues was it?

CHARLIE: I miss him.

FLORA: I think it's terrific.
    What yous have done is terrific.

CHARLIE: I don't know.

FLORA: From the look on your face.
    From the look of you, we did no
    Win, but we did no lose.

CHARLIE: I want to do something.
    I want to apologise.
    Good.
    I want to look after you.
    I could.
    We could.
    I want to do.
    I want to be good.
    I feel.
    We could – together.
    Or something.

    Pause.

FLORA: Terrific.
    That's terrific.

    Pause.

    But you're a loser.
    You's a loser.

CHARLIE: I wanted to explain to you
    What's happened?

FLORA: OK. (*Uninterested.*)

CHARLIE: Your Dad and I. We thought
That if we tried hard enough, we could
Get what we wanted.
I thought that I was –
That I had a special ability to do things.
That I am unique.
The thing is.
I'm not special. Or unique.
I don't have any particular ability
That makes me able to do extraordinary things.
Or to be impressive.
I think I am a bit dangerous.
A nutjob. Or –
I put other people in danger.
People do things they don't want to do.
I think I'm good at making people believe in me.
Of convincing.
I can walk into a room,
And shift people. Twist them.
Even if it hurts them.
I realise.

FLORA: You got it wrong.

CHARLIE: –

FLORA: You got it wrong, giving up.

CHARLIE: We lost.

FLORA: You're making a mistake.
You've given up.
You're like the Lairds who come
And make us play the Highland Games.
With ribbons in my hair
And sing a song for Scotland.

Cringe.

CHARLIE: I don't mind songs.
     They're nice.
     I find them comforting.
     When I was walking and walking to find you.
     I sang some songs to myself.

FLORA: Sing like a happy scot.
     About the land. Or fuckin – heather.

CHARLIE: It is beautiful.

FLORA: It's grey and brown and green.
     I'm no singing about that.
     I can no marry a loser.
     I want to get stuck in.
     You did no take five thousand to the knackers yard.
     They took themselves.
     They should have been more hard core.
     They should have killed every prick standing.
     They should have cashed in victory to themselves.

CHARLIE: Don't you miss your Dad?

FLORA: No.

CHARLIE: He loved you.

FLORA: No I don't.

CHARLIE: He talked about you all the time.
     His Flora.

FLORA: You're a loser.

CHARLIE: He loved you both.

FLORA: Fuck that.
     Fuck that.
     People let you down and then.
     You're naïve.

I find you naïve Charlie.
You look like my Dad's widow.
Maybe you shouldn't have liked him so
much.
Maybe you should have focused on winning.
Maybe you should've been more professional.
We watched you two before you left.
I followed you in the hills.
Talking and chatting.
He talked about you.
All the men talked about you.
Clans came to meet you.
Everyone fuckin loved you.
My Pops loved you.
They done it for you.
Instead of for themselves.
You don't understand revolution.
People need to suit themselves.
There can no be top dogs, in charge
Or speeches.
People with fuckin, badges.
You walked and talked until 3 a.m.
And when he came home to pack his bag
It was like there was a light on.
Like he was in love.

CHARLIE: He got into the idea of it.

FLORA: You're such a loser.

CHARLIE: I wanted to come here and
    Look after you.
    I feel ashamed.
    For trying so hard.
    And the risk.
    People's lives.

FLORA: I don't think that's true.

Everywhere I look there are

Losers.

It's terrific.

People here aren't what they say they are

Don't do what they say they'll do

Talk about how things should be

Do the same thing every day.

I try and stop myself doing the same thing every day.

I try and leave the house backwards or jump

Or sing while getting dressed just so I can

Never say, today was the same old shite as yesterday.

CHARLIE: Your Dad would want me.

To tell you to – .

To explain that you're too young.

And you misunderstand.

Tell me your –

FLORA: Plan?

CHARLIE: There's a plan?

FLORA: You'll ruin it.

CHARLIE: I've got nowhere to go.

FLORA: When you were away,

It was –

he turned thirty.

I lit a fucking birthday candle for him and imagined the men.

My mother just sat there. Excluded. Sat there. Where you are. Sat, sitting.

I imagined the rebels

Hiding in a wood. Or whatever rebels do, you know.

I don't fuckin know.

I made a wish, I wish to be with the rebels.

Are there any left?

CHARLIE: I don't know.
   Maybe a few.

FLORA: Where? In the hills?

   Pause.

FLORA: I know their kids.
   Since the men have been away.
   The children have started chatting.
   Something is going to happen.
   We don't need a prefect.

CHARLIE: They'll be hurt.

FLORA: I'll find the ones
   Who are fast and small and naughty.
   We'll laugh at all of you.
   It will be terrific and funny as fuck.

CHARLIE: You can't make children fight.

FLORA: I am a child.
   We will be fighting for ourselves.
   Yous have fucked it up.

CHARLIE: Children will get killed.

FLORA: It'll be terrific.

   Pause.

See my thing will be an upgrade on yours.
It'll be terrific.
If you had died down there.
I'd want to be with you.
I'd think you were hot.
I'd have a picture of you on my wall.
But no way.
Can't fancy that.

I don't want to be a poem. You can be poem.
I can't fuck a loser.
I can't fuck a poem can I?

CHARLIE: I came here for you.

FLORA: You never believed in shite.

CHARLIE: I DO. I did.

FLORA: If you believed in it.
You'd be dead.
Poem!

FLORA: My Dad believed.

CHARLIE: He believed in me.

FLORA: He believed in a free Scotland.

CHARLIE: He didn't know what that is.

FLORA: He died for it.

CHARLIE: I don't think so.

FLORA: He knew this way of living was bullshit.

CHARLIE: He died because I asked him to.

FLORA: You just said 'die for me'? And he did?

CHARLIE: Yes.

FLORA: –

CHARLIE: Please don't go.

FLORA: I wanted you to be something better.
Never meet your heroes.
That's true.
What a fucking disappointing afternoon this has been.

CHARLIE: I want to repair the – .
Look after you.

FLORA: No, you want to BE me.
　　You want to have your time again.
　　You want to get inside my skin
　　And BE me.
　　You want a second go.
　　A happy re-run ever after.

CHARLIE: I'll do what you need.
　　To help you.
　　I owe him.
　　I owe your Pops.
　　I misled him.

FLORA: You didn't. You were right.
　　You just didn't try hard enough.

　　CHARLIE takes out a note.

CHARLIE: I've got a letter from him
　　For you.

FLORA: He could no read.
　　He could no write.

CHARLIE: He asked me to write it down.

FLORA: It's Ok.

CHARLIE: You don't want to read the letter from your
　　Father?

FLORA: It's fine.
　　No.

CHARLIE: He wanted you to read it.
　　Take it.

FLORA: –

CHARLIE: The letter.

　　CHARLIE holds it out to her.

CHARLIE: I'll read it to you.

FLORA snatches it and reads her name on the envelope.

FLORA: Funny writing.

She crumples it.

CHARLIE: Read the message!
Read the fucking message!
Do it! I'm telling you to open it.
It's a message from him.
You want to hear what he wanted to say to you.
Read it.

Silence.

FLORA: No.

Pause.

With you, it would be like
Suffocating myself with my own pillow.
Really, really slowly.
I would consider myself, immature.
Thanks though.
I'll hide you.
I'll take you in the boat as far as Skye.
You can keep the dress.
It looks terrific.

4. HILLS

DONALD and CHARLIE stand apart, outside.

CHARLIE: I can't hear you, because of the wind.

DONALD: I said…

CHARLIE: It's not that I'm not listening.

DONALD: I said… 'no'.

CHARLIE approaches.

DONALD: I have to get back.

CHARLIE: You can see where our boats came in from here.

DONALD: I'm expected back at the house.

Pause.

CHARLIE: Can we talk about the farm?

DONALD: What farm?

CHARLIE: Your farm. The farm you'll have. Down the line.

DONALD: For crops?

CHARLIE: For growing stuff. Crops, whatever, yes.

DONALD: My farm.

CHARLIE: Your farm. Landowner.

DONALD: That would be – . A crop farm.

CHARLIE: It will be nice. WILL be nice.

DONALD: Would you

CHARLIE: / WILL you…

DONALD: Will you be allowed to give me a farm? Could you, can you do that?

CHARLIE: I'll be king.

DONALD: I keep forgetting to call you sir. Or –

CHARLIE: I can visit at weekends, see how you're doing. It'll be nice. Does it sound nice?

DONALD: It sounds nice.

CHARLIE: See?

DONALD: Really?

CHARLIE: It will be.

DONALD: Ha.

CHARLIE: I feel like we're going to be friends.

DONALD: I have to go home.

Pause.

CHARLIE: I told you there's an army I can recruit.

DONALD: –

CHARLIE: It's all set up.
We'll take Edinburgh first.
March the army onto it.
Take it.

DONALD: Oh-aye.

CHARLIE: The way of it.

DONALD: Right.

CHARLIE: I'm a – a, sounds stupid. A pioneer. A modernist. I
think.

DONALD: Oh-aye. What's your way then?

CHARLIE: My way? Oh, um, ostensibly, I'd burn it.

DONALD: Torch it.

CHARLIE: I'd torch the whole thing.
Smash.
Nothing left.
All gone.
What do you think?

DONALD: Me?

CHARLIE: What would you do?

DONALD: If I could do anything?

CHARLIE: You can do anything. But yes.

DONALD: I'd do the same.
Burn it.

CHARLIE: But Stuarts like to keep castles.
So.

Silence.

CHARLIE: Ostensibly… (*Pause.*) Thank you for showing me around. For giving me the tour.

DONALD: No bother.

CHARLIE: When we were walking, you to my right, I don't know if you noticed, sometimes we would accidently fall into step. Like we were marching. A complete accident. One of those funny things, but you look like someone I can work with. A real person. Your legs anyway.

DONALD: OK.

CHARLIE: Did you know my father?

DONALD: He's a bit of a Stuart legend here.

CHARLIE: He said.

DONALD: Never met him. Others did. Apparently. He's well liked.

Pause.

CHARLIE: He didn't win though.

DONALD: They don't usually, ken. I wouldn't judge him on that.

CHARLIE: Wouldn't you? I would. When he came back I thought, 'what are you doing home?' That's what went though my mind, 'back already?' You know.

Pause.

CHARLIE: I'm more open than him.
    To ideas.

Pause.

DONALD: I'm no coming with you. But I am curious. I'm a bit
    suspicious. Why do you want to do this? What's the –

CHARLIE: Objective?

DONALD: No. What are you trying to achieve?

CHARLIE: Sort of... we're calling it. To keep it simple, we've
    agreed to just call it freedom. There's a more complex
    thesis behind it based on a kind of evolution of the
    traditional Stuart ideology, moving into something more
    progressive...

DONALD: / Where is there some less Freedom?

CHARLIE: On the Laird-owned land.

DONALD: Where?

CHARLIE: Here.

DONALD: Here?

CHARLIE: Soon the land will all be Laird-owned and you'll
    lose it.

DONALD: Less Freedom like that.

CHARLIE: Less freedom opportunity to make money.

DONALD: Oh-Aye-Ok.

    It's always been shit here.

CHARLIE: It's not in other parts.

DONALD: Oh-aye. Yeah-well.

CHARLIE: We can make it better for people like you.
    Real people.

Silence.

DONALD: I've not seen much sheep grazing, if you're talking about grazing.

CHARLIE: My Dad says the grazing will come.

DONALD: You don't believe it until you see it do you?

CHARLIE: No.

DONALD: You've painted a nasty picture of life here in a few years. You've made me feel pretty fucking shit about my life. I can tell you. Thanks for that.

CHARLIE: People don't believe things until they happen. They think everything's ok. Then suddenly –
And it's too late.
It's hard to be proactive.
The Jacobites. Are proactive, pre-emptive. Direct.
I feel like a salesman. I don't want to go on about it but...

DONALD: No, I can tell you mean it.

CHARLIE: I do. But still. Going door to door. Selling...

DONALD: Selling freedom.

CHARLIE: Selling the ideas yes.

DONALD: Selling yourself. If you're selling I'm buying!
(*DONALD laughs awkwardly.*)

Silence.

CHARLIE: Do you not want Scotland to be free? Is that something that...

DONALD: / Scotland will be free you mean? Of course I fucking want Scotland will be free, of course I fucking do. Who d'you think I am? I'm a SCOT. I want Scotland will be fucking free. Fuck off.

CHARLIE: You sound unsure.

DONALD: You were talking about happy, and sheep and money and that. Not about Scotland and free like we mean.

CHARLIE: What do you mean?

DONALD: You know – 'Scotland will be free'.
You know.
THAT.

CHARLIE: I think I can...

DONALD: Scotland will be free.

CHARLIE: I think I can make Scotland will be free.

DONALD: OK.

CHARLIE: I should have said.

DONALD: When you said oppression...

CHARLIE: Don't worry, oppressed people never know what 'oppressed' means.

DONALD: When you said 'oppression'. I know what oppression means. What does oppression mean?

CHARLIE: It's that feeling.

DONALD: What feeling?

CHARLIE: That feeling.

DONALD: What?

CHARLIE: Like you're carrying something. No, um. Like you're small. Ostensibly. Like you're very small. And you are walled in. Giant walls... Sorry. I'm nervous. It used to mean 'oppressed' and now it means being vulnerable, volatile all of the time. Not in control. You can't make plans.

DONALD: Plans?

CHARLIE: Everything is too – fragile.

Pause.

DONALD: Do you like it here? People say it's pretty.

CHARLIE looks out, and smiles.

CHARLIE: Most things look ugly to me. I just see all the shit
stuff. I see what it isn't. What it isn't allowed to be because
people are too lazy to change it.
Not the nature, the man stuff.
No, it's pretty.

DONALD: People always say, 'you're lucky to live somewhere
so beautiful'. They always say that.

CHARLIE: Do they?

DONALD: I could no leave it. It gives you something, that's
nothing to do with anything.

Pause.

DONALD: You should… get on.

CHARLIE: I will…

DONALD: You've seen the land now.

CHARLIE: I have.

DONALD: Your Pops will want an update. Your army will want
to be recruited.
I'll take you as far as the marshes.

CHARLIE: Donald…

DONALD: I've got a wife.

CHARLIE: Of course.

DONALD: It's Flora's birthday! I've got to get back.

CHARLIE: Who's Flora?

DONALD: My daughter.

CHARLIE: Maybe it's because I don't have a family. But I don't know…

DONALD: What?

CHARLIE: It comes down to what's important and what's not. What is and what isn't.

DONALD: Flora's everything.

CHARLIE: No.

I mean. No, no.

No. I don't think your daughter is important.

DONALD: What about my wife, my family?

CHARLIE: No.

DONALD: Give yourself a year and you'll be looking for one yourself.

CHARLIE: I won't. It's ideals. They're what counts.

DONALD: You're too young!

CHARLIE: Sorry.

DONALD: You'll change your tune.

CHARLIE: I'm young enough. Isn't that it? You're saying, in a year, I'll see things just like you do. I'll have given up? If that's true, then I've got this tiny, tiny window of opportunity, to even try, I've got to do it now. Or it's too late. I've got what, a year max.

Pause.

Your kid, she's important to you, sure. But she's not important in the scheme of things. For right now. For the what I'm talking about. She's just not.

DONALD: OK!

CHARLIE: A bit grand?

DONALD: I sort of. I don't know. It's OK.

Pause.

(*Laughing reluctantly.*) I like it.

CHARLIE: (*Laughing too.*) Why?

DONALD: I don't know.

CHARLIE: What does it feel like?

DONALD: I don't know. Freeing.

Pause.

CHARLIE: I told my brother, my Dad, everyone I'd do this.
Even I didn't know I could. It's the hardest thing I've ever
decided to do. I nearly wimped out. This close.
I nearly got back on the boat. Fuck it, back to Rome lads!
You make me feel sort of confident.

DONALD: Me?

Pause.

DONALD: I could tell no one I saw you.

CHARLIE: ?

DONALD: You can still go back.

CHARLIE: Ok but if I don't fight Scotland won't ever be free.

DONALD: Scotland will be free. That's what we say.

CHARLIE: You do actually have to fight for that.

DONALD: Scotland will be free.

CHARLIE: It isn't just free.

DONALD: But Scotland will be free.

CHARLIE: You know you sound ignorant. You know that right?

Pause.

CHARLIE: If my Dad had really fouled things up, properly, there'd be nothing to pick up. But there's half an army and half a battle going on. I can step into that. If he'd messed it up worse. If there was nothing left. I'd do something else. Something. But, this is sort of set up. Like a table set for dinner. Unfinished business.

DONALD: Ready to eat.

CHARLIE: Exactly.

DONALD: Ready to go.

CHARLIE: And I can't help but think that we're going to be the group of people, the generation that wipe the table clean. Us for us. Because we have to, it's our duty to – define ourselves.

DONALD: But you're no one of us. No disrespect but you're an Italian Prince.

CHARLIE: I'm just the one starting the fire.

DONALD: Easy for you.

CHARLIE: Exactly. I think rich people should be the ones to start fires. It's a luxury. I'll be the leader because no one else wants to be. I'll take that risk because I can afford to. But this war is my apprenticeship. You have the opportunity to shape me. What you see now won't be the same person in a year's time. It's you who will indoctrinate me, with what matters to you, so by the end of it I'll be the kind of king you need and we'll know exactly what to do. I've got this half-filled note book of ideas and fuckin-diagrams, and bespoke theses, on what action needs to be taken, can realistically occur and within what timeframes. It's brought me this far, but the blank pages are for – . They're ours.

Pause.

My Dad, he told me a story once about this old warlord who hit on a losing streak. Before...

DONALD: Listen…

CHARLIE: Ha… if I can finish.

And he convinced a young soldier to pretend to um, to pretend to surrender. So the enemy took him into their line. And using a tiny sort of dagger. He, stabbed the enemy general out in the fields, in front of thousands of men.

Then of course they killed the young soldier anyway.

Sad.

DONALD: That's terrible.

CHARLIE: It made me sad.

And a waste.

Dishonorable – that's what I thought. Nothing good can come from that.

There's a way to do things. So it's clean and puts other people first. I have to do this. I've said I will. I want to. I've told everyone. I've told everyone I'm going to do this. But it won't be about me. It's for you. You, you, you!

DONALD: Scotland will be free. All Englishmen will perish.

CHARLIE: No, except the ones that back us.

DONALD: All Englishmen will be slaughtered, except the ones that back us. Scotland will be free.

CHARLIE: Don't be anxious Donnie.

DONALD: I'm not anxious.

CHARLIE: Don't be anxious.

DONALD: I'll come.

Silence. (*CHARLIE smiles.*)

DONALD: Scotland will be free.

CHARLIE: Not like that. Properly.

DONALD: Scotland will be free.

CHARLIE: I mean really, actually. Actually free.

DONALD: I'm coming.

CHARLIE: Ha. But you don't know what I mean.

DONALD: What?

CHARLIE: I can show it to you.
I'm serious.

DONALD: Ok.

CHARLIE: It's not a joke.

DONALD: Alright.

CHARLIE: I can show you so much stuff.

DONALD: I thought you'd be pleased.

CHARLIE: I am pleased. I'm really, really pleased.

Pause.

DONALD: I was going to say one thing.

CHARLIE: One thing.

DONALD: I just don't want to come back embarrassed.

CHARLIE: Embarrassed?

DONALD: I don't want people to laugh and say 'what was that?
What the fuck was that about? What a pair of losers'.

CHARLIE: They won't.

DONALD: I don't want to be a joke.

CHARLIE: If they do we can just say…

Silence.

We can say – 'what the fuck have you ever done?
We're taking the risk'.

CHARLIE: What made you change your mind?

DONALD: I don't know.

Silence.

CHARLIE: You've got all these ideals too. Everyone does. Deep
down. Everyone's got a vision, at their core, they know
how things should be. (*Pause.*)
You don't have to be humble or modest with me.

DONALD: Maybe.

Pause.

CHARLIE: I'm sorry. I know you wanted you saying you're
coming… for me to shake your hand, and for the sun
to set suddenly or, yeah. And you want me to make a
speech about religion and politics, that we're standing at
a crossroads of our time, this is the moment that things
will inevitably shift, to put my finger on where we are,
what 1745 is. I can't, it's too confused, too many factors,
too much information to process. I don't know – 1745, is
1801, or 1511, there's nothing special about now. I think the
important part is us… we FEEL like something has to shift,
so I'm going to back us and make it shift.

DONALD: I better go and –

CHARLIE: The thing is not to tell anyone.
Just go and do it.
Tell them when it's done.
Then it's done.
Then say – that was us.

DONALD: We can't roll backwards.
Or make it worse.

CHARLIE: What are you going to tell your kid?

DONALD: Nothing.

CHARLIE: What about your wife?

DONALD: She'll be angry with me if I'm here or if I'm away, if you see what I'm getting at? Other stuff. Domestic stuff.

CHARLIE: Fair enough.

DONALD: If we win…

CHARLIE: Then she'll get it.

DONALD: The higher purpose… yeh.

CHARLIE: This talk only sounds good in a specific context.

DONALD: When you've won?

CHARLIE: Yes.

Pause.

DONALD: My –
she SEES everything.

CHARLIE: She's just a kid.

Pause.

CHARLIE: I'll meet you at the gate.
Don't worry, I'm a –

DONALD: What? The wind…

CHARLIE: Don't worry I was going to say. It sounds stupid now. I was going to say, 'I'm a winner'. I really believe in myself.
If you believe in yourself you can do anything.

Pause.

DONALD: Ok. Terrific.

END

www.ingramcontent.com/pod-product-compliance
Ingram Content Group UK Ltd.
Pitfield, Milton Keynes, MK11 3LW, UK
UKHW020728280225
455688UK00012B/552